The Power of Visualization:

Making Your Dream a Reality

Sofia Edlund

Contents

Chapter One 3
   Overcoming Limitations 3
   How visualization works 4
   You Can Overcome Your Limited Thinking 7

Chapter 2 9
   The Power of Positive Thinking 9
   How should this power be used? 12
   Reaffirming your desired outcomes 13
   Some words on mental rehearsals 15
   Support Your Visualization With Affirmations 18

Chapter Three 19
   Colorful Living 19
   The Psychology Behind Colors 21
   The Color Effect 23
   Meaning of Colors 25

Chapter Four 31
   Your Most Important Tools 31
   When You Experience a Breakthrough 39
   The Ride May Not Be Smooth 41
   What happens next? 43

Chapter Five 45
   Visualization for fitness and health 45
   How to Relax 48
   Meditation can help you visualize 53

Chapter One

Overcoming Limitations

Visualization is a powerful technique that utilizes the power of imagination to make your dreams and goals a reality. Visualization when used the right way have the power to change your environment and circumstances beyond your wildest imaginations. It can cause events to happen, attract love into your life, alter your circumstances and environment and even bring you possessions and money.

Visualization is similar to daydreaming in that you spent much time thinking about that which you need. People have often expressed the feeling that visualization is similar to magic. The truth is that there is no magic involved in visualization; it is a natural process of mental laws and the power of thoughts. And yes it works like magic; just like having your own personal genie!

Visualization is not new. It is not something that somebody somewhere thought up on the spur of the moment. There are people who make use of visualization everyday of their lives without being aware that they are calling on their natural reserves of power to bring goodness into their lives. There is one thing that all successful people have in common; that is the power to attract success into their lives.

How visualization works

It is a fact that your subconscious mind will accept any thought process that you constantly feed it. When this happens there is every probability that your mindset will be changed and this will in the long run affect your habits and actions. This will strategically position you in situations where you meet new people, circumstances and situations.

Our thoughts are imbued with the creative power that will change our lives for good if we let it. Your thoughts will make you attract that which you think about. The thing about the mind is that it has a way of affecting other minds unconsciously. Your thoughts will be unconsciously picked up by the people rightfully positioned to help you achieve your goals and dreams.

You need to accept that we are a part of an omnipotent power through which the universe and everything in it was created. Little wonder why our thoughts materialize. Stop for a moment and ponder on the fact that you are an indivisible part of an omnipotent universal power. Isn't that awesome? This means that your thoughts can indeed come true if you tune to this omnipotent power. It is important to point out now that not all your thoughts will make it towards being a reality; only those thoughts that are focused, well defined and often repeated will come true.

Our thoughts carry with it energy when it is focused and soaked with emotions. There is a change in the balance of the environment that this energy brings that makes things to swing in our favor. Some people have found it useful to focus their thoughts on their current environment or situation and weave events round their circumstance so as to bring about change. To our subconscious mind, it is like watching the same movie over and over again. The positive thing about our thought process is that we can change our reality and create different circumstances to suit our particular situation.

Take note of the word "Reality". It is by changing your thoughts that you can be able to alter your mental image and create another reality that you want. There is nothing supernatural about this process. You are only making use of powers that comes natural to you and everyone else that is smart enough to realize this. All you need is to makes some changes to your world and attitude and your world will be changed and reshaped.

A good example of how you can bring about this change is thinking of what it is you want in a good way. If you drive a small car and would prefer a bigger car for a change, all you need to do is to change your attitude and thoughts. Instead of bemoaning your fate, you can instead choose to visualize yourself driving the bigger car you want. It is as simple as that.

You Can Overcome Your Limited Thinking

You may be quick to point out that there are some things that may be difficult for you to change; at least in the present. You may be right in this line of thought. The crux of the matter is that the limits to using the power of visualization lie with us and not in the power itself. In other words, we are the only thing keeping us from reaching our full potentials.

Many a times we are quick to limit ourselves to our immediate future. We never care to acknowledge that there may be light at the end of the tunnel. We are overwhelmed by our present situation that we find it difficult believing anything good can ever come our way. We limit ourselves through our thoughts and beliefs. We set limits to ourselves to the life we know.

However, the more open minded amongst us has been able dare to think bigger and look beyond their present situations. They have realized that limitations are only in our minds and that we can rise above them if we so choose. Granted, that it may take some time before you begin to see changes but it will happen in small bits and pieces. If you are dreaming on something big, the results will take a little longer to materialize. Bear in mind that the time and efforts you put into this is not wasted. The key is to have patience and faith.

Chapter 2

The Power of Positive Thinking

We have already learned about visualization and its influence in our lives. Now, the main thing is knowing how to make visualization work for you. The thing about visualization is that it's so simple that we can do it almost anywhere. Below are basic guidelines to make creative visualization work for you.

- Define your goal.

- Think, meditate and listen to your intuition. This will make sure that you really desire to attain this goal.

- Ascertain that only good will result from your visualization; for you and for others.

- Sit alone in a quiet place, where you will not be disturbed.

- Relax your body.

- Breathe rhythmically and deeply several times.

- Visualize a clear and detailed mental image of what you desire to get or accomplish.

- In your imagination, use all the five senses of sight, hearing, touch, smell and taste.

- Add desire and feelings into what your mental image.

- Visualize at least twice a day, about 10 minutes each time.

- Persevere with your visualization, day after day, with patience, hope and faith.

- Strive to stay positive, both in thoughts and feelings, and also when you speak.

- During the day, when negative thoughts and doubts arise, replace them with positive thoughts. As each negative thought enters your mind, immediately substitute it with a positive thought.

- Keep an open mind, so that you recognize opportunities and take advantage of them.

- After concluding your visualization session, say attentively and earnestly, "Let everything happen in a harmonious and favorable way for all involved."

- Keep an open mind for ideas, intuition and opportunities. Creative visualization will open doors, but often, you will have to walk in and take action.

- Whenever you can, take action. Don't be passive, waiting for things to happen by themselves.

How should this power be used?

The power of visualization should not only be used for your own good, it should also be used for the good of others. Never for a moment think of misusing this power to desire for things that belong to another. Your power of imagination should be used to create goodness for all involved and must not cause harm to your environment.

There is a probability that your dreams may materialize in an unexpected and sometimes sudden manner. One thing you should be prepared for is for it to happen gradually and naturally. If you dream of making money, it's very unlikely that it will fall from the skies. It will come through natural means such as a new job, promotion, business deal and other likely activities that will earn you money.

We have the mental capacity to change our thoughts and feelings. Our mental images will affect our lives and those of people around us. Through our thoughts we change our lives by changing the way we think and the things we think about. What this means in effect is that we should be careful with thoughts or we may just attract things that we don't really like and our situations may worsen for it.

Be sure that what you visualize is what you really need. The best way to approach this mental work is by having positive attitude, earnestness and faith. Don't put all your hope on it so much so that you create a state of tension within yourself. Go about it with some amount of detachment. This way you don't feel unnecessarily pressured and feel disappointed if things are not going the way you expect. Some things just take some time to happen.

Reaffirming your desired outcomes

What you have inside of you is a power so awesome that it can affect your world even though you have never been taught how to use it. High performing elite athletes use it.

The peak performers in almost all spheres of human endeavors use this technique to attract and drive success in their lives. One of the fastest ways to accelerate your goals and make them become an overwhelming reality is by visualizing your goals and act as if you have them at your fingertips. There are four very important things that visualization does for you.

- Your creative subconscious is activated and this will lead to creative ideas that will help you achieve your set goals.
- If anything, your brain will readily learn to perceive and recognize resources that you can easily tap into in order to actualize your dreams.
- Positive law of attraction will be readily activated; you will be amazed at how people and resources that will change your circumstance will be drawn into your life.

- You will be highly motivated to tackle challenges that will make you get ahead in life and achieve your dreams.

The good thing about visualization is that it can be practiced anywhere; in your sitting room, bedroom, office, or even out in the fields as long as you feel comfortable in that environment.

Some words on mental rehearsals

The process of affirming your goals and imagining success is a form of mental rehearsal. Athletes use it all the time and even right before events. Set aside a few minutes each day; especially first thing in the morning, after prayers or meditation and right before bedtime. These are usually specific times when you are most relaxed and your mind will accept your affirmations more readily. Visualizations will often time take you less than 5 minutes to accomplish on each occasion. Make it a part of your daily routine and it won't come as a surprise when you start reaping the rewards because your life will be so much improved.

One of the best ways that work as far as visualization is concerned is to create a photographic image of yourself with your goals accomplished. You are seeing yourself as if that goal has already been accomplished. If you desire a new home, all you need do is take a mental photography of yourself inside your new home. Visualize how you want your new home to look and how big it is going to be. Imagine yourself going to your local realtor. Imagine that you are sitting in your new sitting room and relaxing on the sofa with a magazine. Just imagine things as you would want them to be. Find the picture of your ideal home and fix yourself into it.

Visualization can work for any goal that you have in mind. Have a good mental picture of your every goal. It won't do for your goals to be fuzzy and not clear cut. You must know what you want and go for it. This is applicable to every goal you have in life; financial, career, recreation, abilities, skills etc. If your plans are more of a long term one, be prepared to put in effort into it to see it come to pass. Just hang in there and don't give up.

Another useful way to continually remind yourself of your goals and reach for it is by writing down your goals on index cards. Your goals can be as numerous or as little as you want them to be. As you write down your goals in your cards, think of all the ways that your plans will work out for good. Put these cards under near your bed and take them with you as you travel. Each morning as you wake up go through your cards and read them to yourself. Before going to bed each night repeat the same procedure; read the card one at a time, close your eyes and see your goals as it is being completed. Visualize your goal completion for at least 15 seconds, then open your cards and repeat the same process with the net card.

Support Your Visualization With Affirmations

When you affirm you are not only evoking a picture but you are already experiencing the reality within yourself. Repeat your affirmations several times a day; this will help keep you focused on your goal, strengthen your motivation and reprograms your subconscious for success. This way, you are arming your inner self with the crew and tools to do whatever it takes to make your goal happen.

It is quite possible to achieve amazing results through the process of writing your goals, visualizing your success on those goals and repeating your affirmations. What these does is to change your beliefs, assumptions and opinions about you as the most important person in your life. You are harnessing the billions of cells in your brain to achieve what you want. The totality of you is working in a singular and purposeful direction.

Repeat your affirmations every day until you see the completion of that goal and then channel your efforts into another goal. When you positively visualize, you are making it an automatic part of your thinking process that will be woven into every fabric of your being. The key to making this happen is YOU.

Chapter Three
Colorful-Living

As was mentioned in previous chapters, there are many uses of visualization. The only thing restricting you from using this powerful tool to achieve success is you. You can use this wonderful technique to learn new skills, get involved in motivational training, boost self-esteem, and deal with anxiety and stress as well as increase confidence.

In using visualization, all your senses come into play. You use your senses of sight, sound, touch and smell to create the reality you want. You may want to remain in the present while you use your imagination to your advantage. If you can move parallel to the images you create, you will be better able to come to terms with your new found reality. It is also important to consider speed factor if your expectations are to manifest faster. What this means is that you may want to think about the time frame within which you expect your dreams to be accomplished. On the other hand, if you are learning new skills, it may not be a bright idea to proceed at the speed of lightening. You may want to slow things down a bit as you allow yourself to learn as you go. For example, if your new skill involves learning some new technology, you may want to go easy on the speed at which you visualize yourself getting done with the learning curves. It is far preferable to lower your rate of movement so that you can concentrate on visualizing and understand how things are done.

Concept-of-individualism

Your visualization process needs to be individualized. It is up to you to decide the shape and content of your scenes. You are the one that will determine the scene that will work best for you. It lies on you to fashion out scenes and the manner in which you will succeed. When you have found your perfect scene, stick to it and visualize about it repeatedly. Your mind will get used to your visions, store it and make it readily available to you on demand.

The-Psychology-Behind-Colors

Life without colors will be a dull one indeed. Imagine life on the planet without all the colors that we take for granted. How would you feel if you were to take a walk in the garden and all you see are shades of black and grey? This for some people would be worse than death. The good news is that colors are not going anywhere soon and they will be there for us to admire for a long time.

Different colors mean different things to us. When we blush, our cheeks grow red to show we are embarrassed. We stop at the red traffic lights and move as the color changes to green. In fact, we are surrounded by colors that our lives would be different without it. Some colors are universally accepted to mean the same things; just as the example of the traffic lights. Despite our deep interactions with colors we barely know much about them. For the purposes of this book we are going to take a look at the medieval meanings of colors before delving right into the issue of colors and afterwards take a look at what colors symbolize.

Gold   -   honor

Silver   -   fidelity

Red   -   courage

Blue   -   piety

Green   -   Youth

Purple   -   royal

Orange   -   endurance

Black – mourning

The-Color-Effect

Since the dawn of time, color has held special meaning to man. It is no secret that people associate special meanings to certain colors. Nations design their flags based on what colors are most important to them. As time goes on, the meaning of colors has been passed down through generations. In some instances, we associated particular colors to ourselves and thus they become personal to us.

Some people are more comfortable wearing certain colors than others. Colors that appeal to one person may repel another. Colors are known to represent personality, temperament and appearance.

The truth is that colors carry with them signals. Most times we are not aware of it and will not think much on it. Over the years, research has proven that human beings react the same way to particular colors. Have you ever wondered by colored pictures of the brain has areas that are painted yellow? Yellow represents the area of the brain that is in charge of hunger and food. It is no wonder that food chain stores like Macdonald have yellow in its logo.

There have been many researches on the concept of color psychology. Multitude of researches has been geared into this area of interest. All researches so far agree that regardless of nationality, age, gender and profession that people feel the same way about the colors red, orange, yellow, green, violet and blue. Colors are ranked in this order: BLUE - RED - GREEN - VIOLET - ORANGE –YELLOW by psychologists. The reason for this is not well known. But let's not bother our heads about it and delve right into the meaning of colors.

Meaning-of-Colors

Here are the perceived meanings of colors already mentioned above. You may find some of the meanings and inferences quite interesting.

YELLOW – positive

In most places of the world, yellow is seen as a positive color. People associate yellow with joy, happiness and warmth. Maybe this probably has to do with the sun and its color. The only exception to this rule is the people of the Middle East that associates the color yellow with illness and hospitals. The most common perception in psychology is that yellow represents nausea and seasickness.

ORANGE – positive

Just like yellow, orange is seen as a positive color. It represents happiness and joy.

RED - doubt

Red is often seen as the color of love. Roses are painted red in books because it is a flower associated with romance and love. However, there are other meanings associated with red. To many, it represents warmth, happiness and health. Red has a wider range of meanings beside the ones mentioned. The most common conception about red is that it represents doubt, anxiety and hatred. That is why there is a phrase about "seeing red".

ROSE - positive

Here we have a color that is globally accepted as having the same meaning. It represents a girl or woman in many climes. Of course we can deduce that this means happiness and fertility.

WHITE - positive

The popular opinion is that white is the color of purity and innocence.

VIOLET - negative

There are a lot of mixed feelings associated with the color violet. These are grief, illness, betrayal, restlessness and unhappiness. Perhaps, the only exception to this rule is in the US where violet is looked upon as symbolizing peace and harmony. In New Zealand, this color is associated with wisdom, pleasure and hatred.

BLUE - positive

blue conveys the feeling of coldness in whatever guise. It also thought to stand for tranquillity and harmony. Some continents like Europe and South/Central Americas associates blue with health.

GREEN - *positive*

Green is primarily associated with peace, health and harmony in color psychology. No wonder hospitals are painted green or have their blinds and windows painted with this color. Even doctors' surgical gowns are from the color green!

BROWN - *doubt*

When we see the color brown, the first thing that comes into the mind is dull and boring or maybe earthy and hot. In some climes like Japan and China, brown represents hatred.

BLACK - *negative*

Sometimes red and black are perceived the same way. We associated black with diseases, accidents and death.

GRAY- *negative*

The gray color is subject to several interpretations. The

most prevailing notions are that it represents sorrow and sadness. On the other hand, some people consider it to mean longevity and wisdom.

COLOR-MESSAGE

You may be wondering why there is much attention on colors in this chapter. Colors serve two levels of importance; both connotative and denotative. The denotative meaning is apparent when we make a distinction between the different shades and hues of colors. It is the connotative meaning that is of the most important. In our daily dealings and discussions, we give meanings to colors and interpret them the way we can. What we have is the use of colors as symbols of our emotions and accomplishments. In our visualizations, associating colors with deeper meanings will make our visualization stronger and more real. Imagine a man that is visualizing getting a date for the weekend. For this dream to seem real to him, he must find a way to associate his intended date with love. He may dream of presenting his date with pink and red roses. We see that his visualizations will seem more real to him as he associates events and object with colors. It makes it all the more real to him. He will have a realistic expectation and a clear view of what he wants all because he was wise enough to give little items in his dreams colors. These colors are only symbolic but they are his reality.

Chapter Four

Your Most Important Tools

One of the most successful books written on how to utilize mind power "Think and Grow Rich" written by Napoleon Hill. In his book, Hill mentioned six faculties that needed to be developed in order for us to achieve resounding success. These faculties are so important that it literarily arms us with the tools we need to achieve our dreams.

If there is anything that highly successful people have in common, it is highly developed mental faculties that supersedes the need for our five basic senses. Permit me to share with you some of the points raised by Hill on the six senses that needed to be developed. Perhaps, we can also arrive on why this is important and how to go about it.

1. **Reason**

It is a no brainer that our reasoning faculty is what enables us to think. Thinking here means just that; reflecting very deeply on issues. Reasoning does not mean the way you react. You use your brain and think over issues before accepting them as truth. By this you reflect deeply on your goals and not what others think may be good for you.

The mass media has a very strong hold on majority of people but you can stand out from the crowd and refuse to let yourself be taken in by the media. Simply refuse to be controlled by the mass media. There are a lot of negative information being proliferated on the media. Stop watching them so they don't control you and in so doing determine vibrations that will emanate from you. Your vibrations will determine your level of awareness.

There is a very little possibility that you will find programs on the airways that will raise your level of consciousness. Since this is not going to happen, it is better to desist from spending your time on TVs and radios. If anything, they will only lower your level of consciousness. A more profitable way of spending your spare time would be by reading self-help books and articles that will teach you how to improve your life.

2. **Will**

A popular saying goes like this: "When there is a will, there is a way". This is a very apt description of what will is. Will is your ability to direct your energy and concentration towards one purpose; and you do so consciously.

The best way I know to develop your will is by summoning your ability to concentrate for a long period of time. You may decide to look at an object for a long time and not let anything break your concentration. You focus on the object and control your mind not to wander off on its own. When other thoughts intrude on your concentration, you can gently push it aside and not pay any attention to it; all your focus should be on your object of interest. If you can be able to focus for a long time without breaking concentration, your will becomes stronger. This will help you greatly with your visualization as you will be able to see your desires without interruptions.

3. **Perception**

Your perception is your idea of the world. It determines how you see the world. You have a unique view of life which is quite different from that of others. Our views on life stem from our experiences and beliefs which vary. We all have different views because we see the world from angles unique to ourselves.

It is good to understand that your perception can be wrong. In fact, there is every probability that your perception will always be wrong. Don't be fooled by your perceptions. The best way to look at situations is without expressing strong opinions. This should also be applied to every facet of life. You don't judge people since they are the same as you. If you look closely, you will realize that we are all one.

4. **Memory**

Our memories can either be our greatest allies or our biggest foes. Our memories are very important and it serves a lot of useful purposes. Unfortunately, not many people will allow their memories to be their greatest ally. We can choose to remember your past achievements and glories or we can choose to dwell on past failures and let it take control of our lives. What we decide is invariably up to us. To be the best of what we can, we need to use our memories to our greatest advantage.

5. **Intuition**

This is the ability to see behind the façade and glean at inner truths. The faculty of intuition will serve us well by allowing us read the energies that emanates from other people. This ability is one that is given to everyone but for you to develop it, you must use it effectively.

If you can be able to pick up on the mood or attitude of a person and tell if a person is lying or not, you are using your intuitive faculty. There are so many ways that this faculty can be used. It is useful in almost any facet of life. You can pick up a negative, positive, successful, confused and dull energy just by being intuitive.

Energies emanating from people touch us. It is hard to place our fingers on it and fully describe how we are able to feel such energies. Simply put, it is as if some part of a person you feel his energy is touching you and you immediately know what that person is about. If you are intuitive and encounter a person with no strong opinions, you will be able to cue in to the fact that this person has a very light and neutral energy; which actually may be a good thing. What this means is that this person is not judgmental of you and does not have any beliefs about you. On the other hand, if you come in contact with a person and feel very strong and uncomfortable vibrations emanating from that individual, it is an indication that this person may have many limiting beliefs and may also look at people from a strong ego view point.

The picture painted above will be able to provide some strong clues on how to pick up and interpret different energies from people. If you are to develop and use this faculty, it is good to listen to the body languages of people. Rather than pay heed to every single word coming from their mouth, you can decide to feel that person's energy. Try to understand the vibrations coming from that person; the unspoken words that will make all the difference. This will give you a good idea of what the person is trying to tell you without putting it in words. It will reveal to you whether this person is lying to you or hiding something from you.

6. Imagination

Now, we have talked about this important faculty several times in this book. The faculty of imagination lies on the realms of visualization. This is the way through which you are able to manifest your dreams and desires. If you practice developing your imagination through creative and active visualizations, you will have a clearer vision about your desires. It is more than likely that your dreams and goals will manifest faster this way.

When You Experience a Breakthrough

Let me make it clear here that it is very impossible to achieve higher levels of awareness if you keep searching for answers outside of yourself. You are the key that hold all the answers to your life. All the answers you will ever need are inside of you. You have the ability to raise your standard of living and how you go about achieving results if you only visualize. In this case, visualizations will not come without all the necessary support it needs from your other 5 faculties. In other words, you need your other faculties to be alive and working in tandem with your visualizations.

If you visualize about a goal you want to see accomplished, your body vibrations will radiate with that of your goal. This vibrational response enables you to pick up ideas and thoughts that will lead to a higher level of consciousness. This way you are able to see the small and big picture and arrive at ideas that will help accomplish your goals.

Inspirations come to you when you visualize your goals. This is a result of your unconscious mind letting you know how to achieve your goals. Whatever information your unconscious mind tells you is very important towards the accomplishment of your goals. It pays to listen to your subconscious mind as you visualize and see your dreams being accomplished.

Let's assume you are working on a job that you don't derive satisfaction from. You desire a career change but don't quite know how to reach for the skies and achieve your desires. What you most certainly need at that point in time is to visualize yourself already working your dream job or switching to a better satisfying job.

If you are consistent with your visualization efforts, it will soon be apparent that your conscious mind has transferred this idea into your subconscious mind. Your subconscious mind will in turn give sound ideas on how to achieve your desires and goals. You will have your pick of ideas to choose from and when you swing into action and act on your ideas, you will be able to achieve your goals.

The Ride May Not Be Smooth

The journey to the life that you desire for yourself will not be a smooth one. You are going to encounter some obstacles on your way. The bigger your dreams, the bigger the roadblocks you are likely to meet. Don't ever think for a moment that you are going to have it easy and smooth. Whatever you face on your journey to success, fear not, for you will accomplish your goals. The reason why you may not accomplish your desires at the speed of lightening is because of your comfort zone. You have introduced new vibrations into your life that is quite different from what you are used to. There are now two vibrations that are vying for pre-eminence in your life.

Your new and old vibrations are all there and your subconscious mind will learn to pick the conditioning that mostly reflects what you want. You will be confused at this point as many things will seem to go wrong in your life. It is important to point out that these changes are taking place at the subconscious level of your life. Your mind is trying to adjust to the new vibration you introduced.

If you have set big goals for yourself, expect to have big obstacles on your way. You will need to overcome these obstacles to succeed. Have faith in your ability to surmount any challenge that life may throw you. Do not entertain any fears whatsoever. Your faith will let you overcome all challenges that are in front of you.

What happens next?

If you increase your level of vibration and reach a higher state of awareness, you will notice changes in not only yourself but in the world at large. It will be easier for you to manifest your desires and they will be more centered when you do. Your reaction to the world at large will be quite different from what it used to be. You will react in a less dynamic way and you will literally suffer from little or no mood swings. You will notice that you have become generally accepting, understanding, happy and peaceful.

There are many way in which your life will change for the better. You may have to start new relationships and end old ones. You may decide to do things a little differently from what you are used to. There will be a general change in the quality of life that you live. With all these changes taking place in your life, you will be encouraged to further raise your awareness levels.

Chapter Five

Visualization for fitness and health

Have you ever thought for a moment that visualization can help you maintain a healthy lifestyle and keep fit? The truth is that many people suffer from many health issues which may pose difficult problems for them. If you don't use your mind to find healing, it is going to be a long and arduous journey indeed.

By visualizing, you can make many important and lasting changes to your lifestyle. Your chances of success are assured and you will lead a more fulfilling life afterwards. You can either decide to use visualization as a weight gain or weight loss tool. You only have to visualize your body the way you will like to look. This mental image that you create will be transferred to your subconscious from where it will be made manifest to the physical.

For example if you program your subconscious with a mental image of yourself as a healthier or muscular person, your mind will begin to accept this image of yourself and will work towards accomplishing this dream. If you program your mind to accept the proper images that will improve your overall health, you will begin to notice ways in which to lead a healthy life. You just have to believe in your visualizations. It is just like asking you to believe in yourself. You need to let go of past health challenges or your failures to lose weight or refuted efforts at packing more muscles. You need to start believing in yourself more. Let go of any negative image that comes into your mind. Push such thoughts aside and replace them with something positive. Replace them with mental images of your dream self.

If you wish to have your body at perfect proportions, begin to visualize this dream. Your subconscious mind will work hard towards making it a reality. It will reinforce your body system and encourage it to eat more healthy foods and it will also aid your metabolism and eating habits. If gaining weight so you can pack some muscles is what you want, you will need to visualize yourself with all your muscles in the right places.

Try to think differently about your body. Do not concentrate on the fact that your belly is flabby. Create positive thoughts and stick to it. Only then will your subconscious mind make this a reality. Maybe all you needed is the extra motivation to work hard and this is something that your subconscious mind will supply you with in abundance.

All the vital functions in your body are under the control of your subconscious. It is what is at the root of your good and bad habits. It regulates your muscles and body fat composition. Visualize yourself as lean and muscular as you would like; your subconscious will work with you towards making it a reality. Your mind can be a great partner on your path to health.

How to Relax

Sometimes we become so busy that no matter how hard we try we just cannot slow down and get our subconscious mind to get in tune with our thoughts. The only panacea to this problem is to relax and slow down our speed. Relaxation has a way of making us take our minds off the exterior or outside world as we know it and concentrate on our inner selves. We just need to take some alone time to be with ourselves. This is the best times to visualize and concentrate on the things that matter to us.

Each session of properly done visualization is equivalent to 2 hours of deep sleep. Of course if you wake up you will feel doubly energized and revitalized. If you can learn to manage your time, you will look forward to each session rather than get worked up over time constraints.

Your sessions are best done in locations and at times when you won't be disturbed. Take your phone off the hook, and lock your door to avoid interruption. A comfortable position in your room will always work. Whether you are lying down or sitting down comfortably in a chair, it doesn't matter. What matters is that you are comfortable in your position and you are undisturbed. In case you may be tempted to fall asleep, it is better if you sit just so that you can be able to maintain your focus. Your aim is to tap into your sub-conscious mind and you need to be fully awake in order to do that. This is not the best time to sleep.

Inhale deeply and expel all the air in your lungs completely. Take a breath through your nose with your mouth closed. It should take you about 10 seconds to fill your lungs with air. Be careful not to fill your lungs to capacity so you don't hold your breath for too long. Then exhale slowly through your nose for the following ten seconds.

Each breathing cycle should last no more than 30 seconds. Make sure you complete about 5 cycles before you call it off. You will notice your body and mind getting more relaxed with each breathing in and out.

Once you have been able to reach this state of relaxation, it is time to start your visualizations. Are there images you know that power your emotions? Now is the time to release these images and make them come alive. Your images should be colorful and alive. It should feel as if you are actually at the scene. These scenes should be real to you as much as possible.

If your aim is to be physically fit, you may picture yourself fifteen weeks from now. See yourself walking down the beach down to your favorite spot. You are confident in your new figure and are relaxed. You can keep walking in the beach forever without getting tired; all thanks to your new conditioned body.

Now, while at the beach, you take your clothes off revealing well-toned, muscular and well-conditioned body. You have just bought this brand new red swimming suit which has been lying idle in your closet for some time now. This is your opportunity to show case it and let the world see you in it.

Just when you have stripped yourself at the beach, you are the center of all eyes. You even attract the eye of a member of the opposite sex who smiles at you and you smile back. You feel the need to swim in the water and are able to go up to two hundred yards without feeling tired.

You may also consider doing this:

You may visualize your family and friends complementing you on your new looks. Everyone loves the way you look and would love to be just like you. Imagine these scenes to be taking place right before your very eyes and you are pleased with your accomplishments. Everything you visualize should be happening in real time and not in the future.

Visualization can help you construct almost any scene you desire in your mind. You may see yourself at the peak of health, exercising, socializing, and overcoming a particular illness or shortcoming. In your visualizations, you should try and hear people complimenting you about your achievements. Your mental image should be very real to you.

Here are a few tips help you visualize:

- Set a goal for yourself for what you want to achieve.
- You must really want to achieve your goals
- Visualize yourself achieving your goals
- Make use of positive images at every opportunity

These sessions should be practiced daily and over a period of time, say maybe 15 weeks or more. This will make you become more fulfilled and happier.

Meditation can help you visualize

Meditation has been practiced for a long time. It is purported to have been in practice for over five thousand years. You don't have to belong to any religious organization to utilize meditation to help you visualize. To properly meditate, you will need to develop a high level of mental concentration and a stillness of mind. This is very much like the skills needed for visualization.

As I have mentioned previously, you don't have to give up your busy schedule to meditate so you can visualize. All you need to do is find a time that works for you. Meditation is an enjoyable process that is also deeply satisfying. Practice it sometime and you will find it easier to visualize and attract the things that matters most to you.

www.ingramcontent.com/pod-product-compliance
Lightning Source LLC
Chambersburg PA
CBHW041812040426
42450CB00001B/7